IMPRESSION

A CELEBRATION OF LAKELAND SEASONS

£3·50
HRB

CONTENTS

Front Cover – Crummock Water. Back Cover – The Central Massif
Facing page 3 – Langdale Pikes. Facing page 5 – Loughrigg Tarn
Facing page 19 – Wasdale. Facing page 31 – Derwentwater
Facing page 45 – Deepdale. Facing page 59 – Great Gable

MICHAEL PEARSON/RICHARD WARNER

INTRODUCTION

Lakeland, with its indescribable charm and constantly changing atmosphere, has a long association with writers and artists. Many people have attempted to express its unique character through words, prose or poetry and this book has been designed to blend various pieces of inspired descriptive verse with superb photographs.

With one exception, all the authors have had Lakeland associations, but we confess to including, for the most part, pieces by James Thomson. Although there is no evidence of his dwelling in Lakeland, he was brought up not far away, in the borders, moving to Edinburgh before settling in London, and certainly gained a great deal of inspiration from the Welsh mountains and the Alps. Born in 1700, James Thomson was perhaps the first real romantic nature poet to emerge during the eighteenth century, using a wonderful flowing descriptive style, subsequently being used by later writers. His work "The Seasons" was the inspiration behind an audio-visual show produced by "Mikes-eye" which was seen by many visitors to Keswick in 1989. The success of this show was largely the reason for producing this book, which we hope will show Lakeland's infinite charm, combined with suitable and wonderfully expressive words by gifted writers.

SPRING

Bluebell wood

Nor only through the lenient air this change
Delicious breathes; the penetrative Sun,
His force deep-darting to the dark retreat
Of vegetation, sets the steaming power
At large, to wander o'er the vernant earth
In various hues; but chiefly thee, gay green!
Thou smiling Nature's universal robe!
United light and shade! where the sight dwells
With growing strength and ever-new delight.

James Thomson (1700-1748)

SPRING

St. Herbert's Island, Derwentwater

Snatched through the verdant maze, the hurried eye
Distracted wanders; now the bowery walk
Of covert close, where scarce a speck of day
Falls on the lengthened gloom, protracted sweeps;
Now meets the bending sky, the river now
Dimpling along, the breezy ruffled lake,
The forest darkening round, the glittering spire,
The ethereal mountain, and the distant mass.
But why so far excursive? when at hand,
Along these blushing borders bright with dew,
And in yon mingled wilderness of flowers,
Fair-handed Spring unbosoms every grace-
Throws out the snow-drop and the crocus first.....

James Thomson (1700-1748)

Snowdrops

SPRING

Coniston Water

"Cloud on Old Man of Coniston"
Behind it, westward and seaward, all's clear; but when
the wind out of that blue clearness comes over the
ridge of the earth-cloud, at that moment and that line,
its own moisture congeals into these white - I believe,
ice-clouds; threads and meshes, and tresses, and
tapestries, flying, failing, melting, reappearing;
spinning and unspinning themselves, coiling and
uncoiling, winding and unwinding, faster than eye or
thought can follow: and through all their dazzling
maze of frosty filaments shines a painted window in
palpitation; its pulses of colour interwoven in motion,
intermittent in fire, emerald and ruby and pale purple
and violet melting into a blue that is not of the sky,
but of the sunbeam;- purer than the crystal, softer
than the rainbow, and brighter than the snow.

John Ruskin (1819-1900)

Evening sky, Harter Fell

SPRING

Here, by the vocal woods and waters lulled,
And lost in lonely musing, in a dream
Confused of careless solitude where mix
Ten thousand wandering images of things,
Soothe every gust of passion into peace-
All but the swellings of the softened heart,
That waken, not disturb, the tranquil mind.
Behold yon breathing prospect bids the Muse
Throw all her beauty forth. But who can paint
Like nature? Can imagination boast,
Amid its gay creation, hues like hers?
Or can it mix them with that matchless skill,
And lose them in each other, as appears
In every bud that blows?

James Thomson (1700-1748)

Grasmere

SPRING

Ullswater near Glencoyne

When we were in the woods beyond Gowbarrow Park we saw a few daffodils close to the water-side. We fancied that the lake had floated the seeds ashore, and that the little colony had so sprung up. But as we went along there were more and yet more; and at last, under the boughs of the trees, we saw that there was a long belt of them along the shore, about the breadth of a country turnpike road. I never saw daffodils so beautiful. They grew among the mossy stones about and about them; some rested their heads upon the stones, as on a pillow, for weariness; and the rest tossed and reeled and danced, and seemed as if they verily laughed with the wind, that blew upon them over the lake; they looked so gay, ever glancing, ever changing.

Dorothy Wordsworth (1771-1855)

Daffodil

SPRING

Derwentwater near Stable Hills

...this leads me to the mountain-brow
Where sits the shepherd on the grassy turf,
Inhaling healthful the descending sun.
Around him feeds his many-bleating flock,
Of various cadence; and his sportive lambs,
This way and that convolved in friskful glee,
Their frolics play. And now the sprightly race
Invites them forth; when swift, the signal given,
They start away, and sweep the massy mound
That runs around the hill.....

James Thomson (1700-1748)

SPRING

River Brathay and Skelwith

From the moist meadow to the withered hill,
Led by the breeze, the vivid verdure runs,
And swells and deepens to the cherished eye.
The hawthorn whitens; and the juicy groves
Put forth their buds, unfolding by degrees,
Till the whole leafy forest stands display'd
In full luxuriance to the sighing gales-
Where the deer rustle through the twining brake,
And the birds sing concealed. At once arrayed
In all the colours of the flushing year
By Nature's swift and secret-working hand,
The garden glows, and fills the liberal air
With lavish fragrance...

James Thomson (1700-1748)

SPRING

Black Combe from Harter Fell

Meantime you gain the height, from whose fair brow
The bursting prospect spreads immense around;
And, snatched o'er hill and dale, and wood and lawn,
And verdant field, and darkening heath between,
And villages embosomed soft in trees,...
your eye excursive roams-
Wide-stretching from the Hall in whose kind haunt

The hospitable Genius lingers still,
To where the broken landscape, by degrees
Ascending, roughens into rigid hills
O'er which the Cumbrian mountains, like far clouds
That skirt the blue horizon, dusky rise.

James Thomson (1700-1748)

SPRING

Helvellyn from Grey Knotts

There is a power to bless
In hillside loneliness-
In tarns and dreary places-
A virtue in the brook,
A freshness in the look
Of mountains' joyless faces-
And so, when life is dull

Or when my heart is full
Because my dreams have frowned,
I wander up the rills
To stones and tarns and hills-
I go there to be crowned.

F.W. Faber (1814-1863)

SPRING

Meantime, refracted from yon eastern cloud,
Bestriding earth, the grand ethereal bow
Shoots up immense; and every hue unfolds,
In fair proportion running from the red
To where the violet fades into the sky.
Here, awful Newton, the dissolving clouds
Form, fronting on the sun, thy showery prism;
And to the sage-instructed eye unfold
The various twine of light, by thee disclosed
From the white mingling maze.

James Thomson (1700-1748)

Watendlath Tarn and Ullscarf

SPRING

Near Hartsop, Brothers Water

....There along the dale
With woods o'erhung, and shagged with mossy rocks
Whence on each hand the gushing waters play,
And down the rough cascade white-dashing fall
Or gleam in lengthened vista through the trees,
You silent steal; or sit beneath the shade
Of solemn oaks, that tuft the swelling mounts
Thrown graceful round by Nature's careless hand,
And pensive listen to the various voice
Of rural peace- the herds, the flocks, the birds,
The hollow whispering breeze, the plaint of rills,
That, purling down amid the twisted roots
Which creep around, their dewy murmurs shake
On the soothed ear....

James Thomson (1700-1748)

A Lakeland waterfall

SPRING

Rydal Water from Nab Scar ridge

Then spring the living herbs, profusely wild,
O'er all the deep-green earth, beyond the power
Of botanist to number up their tribes:
Whether he steals along the lonely dale
In silent search; or through the forest, rank
With what the dull incurious weeds account,
Bursts his blind way; or climbs the mountain-rock,
Fired by the nodding verdure of its brow.

James Thomson (1700-1748)

SPRING

Rydal Water and Loughrigg

I sate a long time to watch the hurrying waves, and to hear the regularly irregular sound of the dashing waves. The waves round about the little island seemed like a dance of spirits that rose out of the water, round its small circumference of shore.

Dorothy Wordsworth (1771-1855)

SUMMER

Rydal Water

Contentment walks the sunny glade,
And feels an inward bliss spring o'er the mind,
Beyond the power of kings to purchase.
Pure serenity apace induces thought,
And contemplation still.

James Thomson (1700-1748)

SUMMER

Buttermere and Burtness Combe

Thou, like the harmless bee, mayst freely range
From mead to mead bright with exalted flowers,
.....Mayst wander now
Through palmy shades and aromatic woods
That grace the plains, invest the peopled hills,
And up the more than Alpine mountains wave.
There on the breezy summit, spreading fair
For many a league, or on stupendous rocks,
That from the sun-redoubling valley lift,
Cool to the middle air, their lawny tops,
Where palaces and fanes and villas rise,
And gardens smile around and cultured fields,
And fountains gush, and careless herds and flocks
Securely stray- a world within itself,
Disdaining all assault....

James Thomson (1700-1748)

Honeysuckle

SUMMER

Windermere from Todd Crag

A dreary moor
Was crossed; a bare ridge clomb, upon whose top
Standing alone, as from a rampart's edge,
I overlooked the bed of Windermere,
Like a vast river, stretching in the sun.
With exultation, at my feet I saw
Lake, islands, promontories, gleaming bays,
A universe of Nature's fairest forms
Proudly revealed with instantaneous burst,
Magnificent, and beautiful and gay.

William Wordsworth from "The Prelude"

SUMMER

Which way, ... shall we bend our course?
The choice perplexes. Wherefore should we choose?
All is the same with thee. Say shall we wind
Along the streams? or walk the smiling mead?
Or court the forest glades?....

James Thomson (1700-1748)

Borrowdale from King's How

SUMMER

Borrowdale from Sprinkling Tarn

.....or wander wild
Among the waving harvests? or ascend,
While radiant Summer opens all its pride,
Thy hill, delightful hill? Here let us sweep
The boundless landscape.

James Thomson (1700-1748)

Skiddaw and Keswick from Grange Fell

Skiddaw shews its vast base, and bounding all that part of the vale, rises gently to a height that sinks the neighbouring hills; opens a pleasing front, smooth and verdant, smiling over the country like a gentle generous lord, while the fells of Borrowdale frown on it like a hardened tyrant.

Thomas Pennant (1726-1798)

The "jaws" of Borrowdale

SUMMER

Back o' Skiddaw

Behold, slow settling o'er the lurid grove
Unusual darkness broods, and, growing, gains
The full possession of the sky....
How changed the scene! In blazing height of noon,
The sun, oppressed, is plunged in thickest gloom.
Still horror reigns, a dreary twilight round,
Of struggling night and day malignant mixed.
For to the hot equator crowding fast,
Where, highly rarified, the yielding air
Admits their stream, incessant vapours roll,
Amazing clouds on clouds continual heaped;
Or whirled tempestuous by the gusty wind,
Or silent borne along, heavy and slow,
With the big stores of steaming oceans charged.

James Thomson (1700-1748)

Tewit Tarn, Low Rigg near Keswick

SUMMER

....Wide-rent, the clouds
Pour a whole flood; and yet, its flame unquenched,
The unconquerable lightning struggles through,
Ragged and fierce, or in red whirling balls,
And fires the mountains with redoubled rage....
As from the face of heaven the shattered clouds
Tumultuous rove, the interminable sky
Sublimer swells, and o'er the world expands
A purer azure. Nature from the storm
Shines out afresh; and through the lightened air
A higher lustre and a clearer calm
Diffusive tremble;...

James Thomson (1700-1748)

Coledale Fells

Coledale Fells and Derwentwater

SUMMER

Grasmere and slopes of Heron Pike

....while, as if in sign
Of danger past, a glittering robe of joy,
Set off abundant by the yellow ray,
Invests the fields, yet dropping from distress.
The sun has lost his rage: his downward orb
Shoots nothing now but animating warmth
And vital lustre; that with various ray,
Lights up the clouds, those beauteous robes of
   heaven,
Incessant rolled into romantic shapes,
The dream of waking fancy!

James Thomson (1700-1748)

Clouds from Helm Crag

SUMMER

Rich is thy soil, and merciful thy clime;
Thy streams unfailing in the summer's drought;
Unmatched thy guardian-oaks; thy valleys float
With golden waves; and on thy mountains flocks
Bleat numberless; while, droving round their sides,
Bellow the blackening herds in lusty droves.
Beneath, thy meadows glow, and rise unequalled
Against the mower's scythe.

James Thomson (1700-1748)

Gatesgarth near Buttermere

Coledale fells from Millbeck

SUMMER

River Derwent, Borrowdale

Hence let me haste into the mid-wood shade,
Where scarce a sunbeam wanders through the gloom,
And on the dark green grass, beside the brink
Of haunted stream that by the roots of oak
Rolls o'er the rocky channel, lie at large
And sing the glories of the circling year.

James Thomson (1700-1748)

AUTUMN

Brandelhow

Fair Autumn, yellow robed! I'll sing of thee,
Of thy last, tempered days and sunny calms;
When all the golden hours are on the wing.
Now see the fading many-coloured woods,
Shade deepening over shade, the country round
Imbrown; a crowded umbrage, dusk and dun,
Of every hue from wan declining green
To sooty dark. These now the lonesome muse,
Low-whispering, lead into their leaf-strown walks,
And give the season in its latest view.

James Thomson (1700-1748)

Ullswater

Meantime the grandeur of thy lofty dome
Far-splendid seizes on the ravished eye.
New beauties rise with each revolving day;...
And there, light shadowing all, a sober calm
Fleeces unbounded the air; whose least wave
Stands tremulous, uncertain where to turn
The gentle current; while, illumined wide,
The dewy-skirted clouds imbibe the sun,
And through their lucid veil his softened force
Shed o'er the peaceful world. Then is the time
For those whom Wisdom and whom Nature charm
To steal themselves from the degenerate crowd,
And soar above this little scene of things-
To tread low-thoughted Vice beneath their feet,
To soothe the throbbing passions into peace,
And woo lone quiet in her silent walks.

James Thomson (1700-1748)

From Loughrigg to Helm Crag

Crummock Water and Grasmoor

About the first week in October, the rich green, which prevailed through the whole summer, is usually passed away. The brilliant and various colours of the fern are then in harmony with the autumnal woods; bright yellow or lemon colour, at the base of the mountains, melting gradually, through orange, to a dark russet brown towards the summits, where the plant, being more exposed to the weather, is in a more advanced state of decay.

William Wordsworth (1770-1850)

Legburthwaite and St. John's in the Vale

...the potent sun elated high,...
Spreads o'er the vale, or up the mountain climbs
Profuse, and drinks amid the sunny rocks,
From cliff to cliff increased, the heightened blaze.

James Thomson (1700-1748)

Rowan berries

Low bend the weighty boughs. The clusters clear,
Half through the foliage seen, or ardent flame
Or shine transparent; while perfection breathes
White o'er the turgent film the living dew.

James Thomson (1700-1748)

... now the day,
O'er heaven and earth diffused, grows warm and high;
Infinite splendour! wide-investing all.
How still the breeze! save what the filmy threads
Of dew evaporate brushes from the plain.

James Thomson (1700-1748)

Crummock Water and Rannerdale Knotts

AUTUMN

Crummock Water

How clear the cloudless sky! how deeply tinged
With a peculiar blue! the ethereal arch
How swelled immense! amid whose azure throned,
The radiant sun how gay! how calm below
The gilded earth!...

James Thomson (1700-1748)

Derwent Valley and Bassenthwaite marshes

Now, by the cool declining year condensed,
Descend the copious exhalations, checked
As up the middle sky unseen they stole,
And roll the doubling fogs around the hill.
No more the mountain, horrid, vast, sublime,
Who pours a sweep of rivers from his sides,
And high between contending kingdoms rears
The rocky long division, fills the view

With great variety; but in a night
Of gathering vapour, from the baffled sense
Sinks dark and dreary. Thence expanding far,
The huge dusk gradual swallows up the plain:
Vanish the woods: the dim-seen river seems,
Sullen and slow, to roll the misty wave.

James Thomson (1700-1748)

River Rothay and Rydal Water

The western sun withdraws the shortened day;
And humid evening, gliding o'er the sky,
In her chill progress, to the ground condensed
The vapours throws. Where creeping waters ooze,
Where marshes stagnate, and where rivers wind,
Cluster the rolling fogs, and swim along
The dusky-mantled lawn.

James Thomson (1700-1748)

AUTUMN

Hoar frost by Bassenthwaite Lake

The lengthened night elapsed, the morning shines
Serene, in all her dewy beauty bright,
Unfolding fair the last autumnal day.
And now the mounting sun dispels the fog;
The rigid hoar-frost melts before his beam;
And, hung on every spray, on every blade
Of grass, the myriad dew-drops twinkle round.

James Thomson (1700-1748)

Near Jenkin Crag, Ambleside

AUTUMN

Grange Fell and Castle Crag

There let me sit beneath the sheltered slopes,
...And, with thy converse blest, catch the last smiles
Of Autumn beaming o'er the yellow woods.
While there with thee the enchanted round I walk...

James Thomson (1700-1748)

Watendlath trees

Now, flaming up the heavens, the potent sun
Melts into limpid air the high-raised clouds
And morning fogs that hovered round the hills
In parti-coloured bands; till wide unveiled
The face of nature shines from where earth seems,
Far-stretched around, to meet the bending sphere.

James Thomson (1700-1748)

Castle Head and Skiddaw

Wythop Woods

AUTUMN

Birches on Falcon Crag

Even in the height of noon oppressed, the sun
Sheds, weak and blunt, his wide-refracted ray;
Whence glaring oft, with many a broadened orb,
He frights the nations. Indistinct on earth,
Seen through the turbid air, beyond the life
Objects appear, and, wildered, o'er the waste
The shepherd stalks gigantic; till at last,
Wreathed dun around, in deeper circles still
Successive closing, sits the general fog
Unbounded o'er the world, and, mingling thick,
A formless grey confusion covers all.

James Thomson (1700-1748)

Helvellyn range from Skiddaw

WINTER

Seatoller

See, Winter comes to rule the varied year,
Sullen and sad, with all his rising train-
Vapours, and clouds, and storms. Be these my theme;
These, that exalt the soul to solemn thought
And heavenly musing. Welcome, kindred glooms!
Congenial horrors, hail! with frequent foot,
Pleased have I, in my cheerful morn of life,
When nursed by careless solitude I lived,
And sung of nature with unceasing joy,....

James Thomson (1700-1748)

Pleased have I wandered through your rough domain;
Trod the pure virgin-snows, myself as pure;
Heard the winds roar, and the big torrent burst;
Or seen the deep-fermenting tempest brewed
In the grim evening sky. Thus passed the time,
Till, through the lucid chambers of the south,
Looked out the joyous Spring; looked out, and smiled.

James Thomson (1700-1748)

Tortured larch above Tilberthwaite

WINTER

Lord's Island, Derwentwater

As when a shepherd on a vernal morn thro' some thick fog creeps tim'rous with slow foot, darkling he fixes on th' immediate road his downward eye: all else of fairest kind hid or deform'd. But lo, the bursting Sun! touched by th' enchantment of that sudden beam strait the black vapor melteth, and in globes of dewy glitter gems each plant and tree: on every leaf, on every blade it hangs! dance glad the new-born intermingling rays, and wide around the landscape streams with glory!

S.T. Coleridge (1772-1834)

Jewelled cobweb

Castlerigg Stone Circle

Clouds, mists, streams, watery rocks and emerald turf,
clouds of all tincture, rocks and sapphire sky,
confused, commingled, mutually inflamed, molten
together, and composing thus, each lost in each, that
marvellous array of temple, palace, citadel, and huge
fantastic pomp of structure without name, in fleecy
folds voluminous enwrapped.

William Wordsworth (1770-1850)

Blencathra and Derwentwater

When from the pallid sky the Sun descends,
With many a spot, that o'er his glaring orb
Uncertain wanders, stained; red fiery streaks
Begin to flush around. The reeling clouds
Stagger with dizzy poise, as doubting yet
Which master to obey;...

James Thomson (1700-1748)

Icicles, White Moss Common

Therefore all seasons shall be sweet to thee,
Whether the summer clothe the general earth
With greenness, or the redbreast sit and sing
Betwixt the tufts of snow on the bare branch
Of mossy apple-tree, while the nigh thatch
Smokes in the sun-thaw; whether the eave-drops fall
Heard only in the trances of the blast,
Or if the secret ministry of frost
Shall hang them up in silent icicles,
Quietly shining to the quiet Moon.

S.T. Coleridge (1772-1834)

WINTER

Aira Force, Ullswater

To thy loved haunt return, my happy Muse:
For now, behold! the joyous Winter days,
Frosty, succeed; and through the blue serene,
For sight too fine, the ethereal nitre flies,
Killing infectious damps, and the spent air
Storing afresh with elemental life.
Close crowds the shining atmosphere; and binds
Our strengthened bodies in its cold embrace,

Constringent; feeds, and animates our blood;
Refines our spirits, through the new-strung nerves
In swifter sallies darting to the brain-
Where sits the soul, intense, collected, cool,
Bright as the skies, and as the season, keen.

James Thomson (1700-1748)

WINTER

Derwentwater

....with the fierce rage
Of winter deep suffused, an icy gale,
oft shifting o'er the pool breathes a blue film..
..'Tis brightness all; save where the new snow melts
Along the mazy current...

James Thomson (1700-1748)

Cat Gill near Keswick

WINTER

Great Wood

.....Low the woods
Bow their hoar head; and, ere the languid sun
Faint from the west emits his evening ray,
Earth's universal face, deep-hid and chill,
Is one wild dazzling waste, that buries wide
The works of man.

James Thomson (1700-1748)

Clough Head and Keswick from Whinlatter

Grisedale Pike

In this dire season, oft the whirlwind's wing
Sweeps up the burden of whole wintry plains
In one wide waft, and o'er the hapless flocks,
Hid in the hollow of two neighbouring hills,
The billowy tempest, 'whelms: till, upward urged,
The valley to a shining mountain swells,
Tipped with a wreath high-curling in the sky.

James Thomson (1700-1748)

WINTER

Blencathra and slopes of Latrigg

On stern Blencathra's perilous height
The winds are tyrannous and strong;
And flashing forth unsteady light
From stern Blencartha's skiey height,
As loud the torrents throng!

S.T. Coleridge (1772-1834)
A Thought (suggested by a view of saddleback)

WINTER

Grasmere

A Stranger, Grasmere, in thy vale,
All faces then to me unknown,
I left my sole companion-friend
To wander out alone.

Lured by a little winding path,
Quickly I left the publick road,
A smooth and tempting path it was
By sheep and shepherds trod.

Eastward, towards the lofty hills
That pathway led me on
Until I reach'd a stately rock
With velvet moss o'ergrown.

With russet oak, and tufts of fern
Its life was richly garlanded;
Its sides adorned with eglantine
Bedropped with hips of glossy red.

Beneath that Rock my course I stayed,
And, looking to its summit high,
'Thou wear'st', said I, 'a splendid garb,
Here winter keeps his revelry.

What need of flowers? the splendid moss
Is gayer than an April mead,
More rich its hues of varied green,
Orange and gold and glowing red.'

Beside that gay and lovely Rock
There came with merry voice
A foaming Streamlet glancing by:
It seemed to say 'Rejoice!'

My youthful wishes all fulfill'd-
Wishes matured by thoughtful choice,
I stood an Inmate of the vale,
How could I but rejoice?

Dorothy Wordsworth (1771-1843)

Mossy stream

WINTER

Derwentwater from Walla Crag

And now am I a Cumbrian mountaineer;
Their wintry garment of unsullied snow
The mountains have put on, the heavens are clear,
And yon dark lake spreads silently below;
Who sees them only in their summer hour
Sees but their beauty half, and knows not
Half their power.

Robert Southey (1774-1843)

INDEX OF AUTHORS

PHOTOGRAPHS

by Mike Pearson except for Andy Warner (back cover) and Richard Warner 15 (bottom), 28 (top), 29, 35, 44, 46, 51, 53 (top), 55, 58.

NOTES

Mike Pearson, one half of the "Mikes-Eye" partnership, moved to Keswick from York over 20 years ago and has produced audio-visual slide/tape programs for an even longer period of time. Subsequent employment at Whinlatter Visitor Centre gave the opportunity to use twin projection techniques and it is largely due to the encouraging response from audiences that in 1985 he joined forces with Richard Warner and started producing postcards and greetings cards of Lakeland scenes under the Mikes-eye name.

In 1977 Richard Warner, then a design engineer, escaped the clamour of the home counties and, with the entire Warner 'clan', moved north to Keswick. For the first nine years the dream of living in the Lake District was sustained by Strathmore guest house and his photography now being called upon originates mainly from this era. When the time came to leave the guest house the family moved to Wythop and Richard was given the opportunity to join Mike at the Visitor Centre.

Designed by Stephen England

First published in 1990 by "Mikes-eye", Riggs House, Routenbeck, Wythop Mill, Cockermouth, Cumbria

British Library classification
ISBN 0 9516220 0 5

Made and printed in Cumbria, Great Britain by Frank Peters (Printers) Ltd.